About The Author

Nicholaus Carpenter is one of the most sought after thought leaders and marketing coaches in the mortgage and real estate industries. He is the founder of The Legion of Loan Officers, America's mastermind for smart mortgage professionals, teaching Mortgage Brokers and Retail Lenders how to add 10 Realtor partners in less than 90 days using the Agent Attraction System. Carpenter has taught hundreds of Realtors and thousands of lenders across America and Canada. He invites you to visit his company's website at http://legionofloanofficers.com.

Page One Takeover: How Mortgage Brokers and Real Estate Agents Can Dominate Google with YouTube Videos

Nicholaus Carpenter

Copyright © 2013-2020
Nicholaus Carpenter

Paperback was first published in 2020.
EBook originally published in 2013.

To Stewart for telling me I was a six figure man with no product back in 2011. It was the push I needed. Thank you.

Contents

Introduction Page 12

1 | Research Page 17

2 | Create Page 24

3 | Publish Page 29

4 | Connect Page 35

5 | Promote Page 40

Conclusion Page 42

Bonus Strategy Page 44

Page One Takeover: How Mortgage Brokers and Real Estate Agents Can Dominate Google with YouTube Videos

1. Research
2. Create
3. Publish
4. Connect
5. Promote

$ $ $
$ $

Introduction

Everybody wants to be on the first page of Google, right?

The reality is that it is not necessarily a super easy thing to do, but it can be very simple. In fact, I find that it's much easier to get a video on the first page of Google than it is to get text on the first page.

That's why I focus my effort on videos.

Check out some of these results:

Google | johnson place southlake tx

Web Images Maps Shopping Videos More ▼ Search tools

About 421,000 results (0.32 seconds)

Johnson Place
www.tollbrothers.com/TX/Johnson_Place
Johnson Place is an exclusive **Toll Brothers** community located in the heart of prestigious **Southlake**. Hurry in, nearly sold out! Model Home For Sale
Google+ page · Be the first to review

📍 2304 Top Rail Ln Southlake, TX 76092
(817) 379-4900

Toll Brothers Builders Home Features - **Johnson Place** - New ...
www.youtube.com/watch?v=LcMNdu03z_A
Jun 28, 2010 - Uploaded by Troy George
We went and visited with Ryan Dealey, on site sales in Johnson Place for Toll Brothers Home Builders in ...

Johnson Place - Southlake **Tx** 76092 - Homes Ohio

Google | spyglass hills keller

Web Images Maps Shopping Videos More ▼ Search tools

About 488,000 results (0.49 seconds)

1505 **Spyglass Hill** Dr, **Keller**, TX 76248 - Zillow
www.zillow.com › Texas › Keller › 76248
View pictures, the sales history and details about the Zestimate value of $568728 for 1505 **Spyglass Hill** Dr.

1516 **Spyglass Hill** Dr, **Keller**, TX 76248 - Zillow
www.zillow.com › Texas › Keller › 76248
View pictures, the sales history and details about the Zestimate value of $438354 for 1516 **Spyglass Hill** Dr.

Spyglass Hill Estates in **Keller**, Texas Video Tour - Custom Homes ...
www.youtube.com/watch?v=CwOtysDr_i4
Oct 29, 2010 - Uploaded by Troy George
http://goo.gl/HQ3T **Spyglass Hill** Estates in **Keller**, Texas features 27 functional home lots with rolling land and ...

Spyglass Hill Estates - Dallas Custom Homes | Fort Worth Custom ...

My name is Nick Carpenter and I'm an Air Force veteran turned real estate agent back in 2005. I had some success with the largest independent real estate company in Dallas Fort Worth and went on to win Rookie of the Year in 2006.

Around that time, 2006-2007, I was discovering that there were some ways to generate leads online that most real estate salespeople were not utilizing.

It was around then I realized I have a passion for real estate and marketing – but not necessarily taking buyers in my car and showing homes.

I'm more of the fisherman. I love the chase and the hunt. Some people would call that person a rainmaker.

This process led me to my love of video and using video to drive business for other people.

The 5-step process you're going learn in this book will help you shoot a video and get that video found by Google and

YouTube so more people can hear your message.

Before we really jump into the process I need to cover something that cripples so many people –

VIDEO SHYNESS

The thing I share with my clients, like Realtors and Loan Officers, is whoever you are, that's just who you are. If you've got a pimple or if you're not dressed in a suit one day, that's just who you are. (Look at this picture when I was at my WORST HAIR DAY and kept on making videos!)

When you jump on video, whoever you are, that's what people are going to meet when they come to you in person. So why not just let them meet you before they get there?

They'll know you better; they'll feel like they have a relationship with you already, and it just builds up credibility.

The average person is consuming 2 to 3 hours of videos a month.

Everybody is watching videos, but people are still a little nervous to jump in front of a camera and shoot their own content.

Why?

Feel the fear and do it anyways.

Alright so let's jump into this 5 step process for Google Domination. Parenthesis

Chapter 1 | Research

The first thing that we teach people to do is that they absolutely have to do, it's so critical, is that you have to do the research.

You have to know what people are searching on Google!

As opposed to being a salesperson, a lot of times we get caught up in our own world and we have an idea of what we want to bring to people. But maybe that's not necessarily what they're looking for.

The tool I recommend people use is called the Google Keyword Tool. You need to be logged into a Google Ads account to use it but it's free.

You can search that on Google and it will be there.

It was really made for advertisers to know what people are searching for, so you could see how many times a month people in America are searching a certain term.

You can see what the competition is out there from an advertising perspective and you won't have to waste your time and your marketing efforts on doing something that people aren't even looking for.

The other thing that is great about doing your research is you can laser focus on a niche and you can get that "hyper local" content going with what people in your market are searching for.

With the Google Keyword Tool I can figure out what my target market is searching for and I can bring that content to them.

I eliminate so much of the process of trying to get people to my stuff, trying to get people to blog, my website – because I'll just give them what they want.

I help them to get to my site easier through that process by doing the research.

We're going to talk about shooting the videos and all that. Of course the message matters when you're shooting a video. The content matters because ultimately, you want to be providing good value.

When you do your research and your SEO, when you keyword your video and do things I'm going to show you, that's how people will find your awesome content.

The research and the work that you are going to do upfront is what will get people there, not the content that is on the video.

When I'm doing research and looking through the Google Keyword Tool I'm trying to figure out about 5 to 10 different keyword phrases we can do at a time.

I'm looking for a "search sweet spot", which I call it the area between 500 and 1500 searches per month.

The reason I call it a sweet spot is that big blogs and big companies and things like that are not necessarily going to go after the search only 1000 people are looking for a month. But if you can get an extra 1000 people on your website, that is HUGE!!

If you're a Realtor, loan officer, insurance agent, network marketing professional, whatever it may be – and you can get a 1000 people on your website every month from one search term, it's humongous.

It's such a perfect niche number. It's so much easier to rank because there's no competition.

Let's use real estate as an example - look at the term "real estate". You're competing with Zillow and Trulia and Realtor.com.

When you can go down to a neighborhood level or what people call a "hyper-local" – that's going to be on a neighborhood level, it's going to be even smaller than a city level.

Real Estate Sweet Spot

- City level ZTR
- Neighborhood level ★ Sweet Spot ★
- Property level ZTR

When you can get down to that kind of a level of searching, you're going to find those sweet spots and you're going to have so much easier time getting your videos on Google and driving that traffic because you're not going to be competing with the big box brands.

It's kind of like David and Goliath.

It's so much easier when you can find those little niche searches, the "long tailed keywords".

Long tail keyword just means a whole phrase vs. one word. If "real estate" is a short phrase than "Arlington TX pool homes for sales" is a "long tail keyword".

See the difference there?

You want to find those complete phrases that you can go after.

This same type of research can be done on YouTube also.

Go over and search the phrases you want to rank for and see the competition. I like to search the phrases normally and with quotation marks around it.

There's a free Google Chrome Extension that will show you the backend of any video on YouTube.

You'll see the keyword tags and all the video info.

The extension is called VidIQ. They have free and paid versions but the free one is plenty powerful for most people.

Chapter 2 | Create

The next step is to shoot your video. Would it be ok if I give you a couple of ideas how you can do that.

I'm not going to tell you to go buy a $1,000 camera and a $100 microphone and $1,000 video editing software.

Today you don't need that stuff until you get really consistent with making content.

The simplest for a lot of people that have a laptop is to use the webcam.

You're going to record it directly onto your computer.

You can also do it right through your smart phone.

I use an iPhone personally, and other people prefer the Android. These phones take better pictures and videos than a lot of cameras out there today.

You don't need to go out and buy a bunch of expensive equipment.

The cell phone you have in your pocket can probably suffice for exactly what you need.

Today, audio quality is very important.

If you create a video with bad audio, people are not going to listen to your video. There are too many options out there, there are too many choices – and they'll go find somebody that took the time to make good quality audio and they're going to listen to that.

Samson makes a really nice lavaliere microphone made for specifically cell phones.

How long should videos be?

As long as necessary and as short as possible.

I try to keep my Facebook videos under 3 minutes and my YouTube videos less than 15 minutes.

Every video doesn't have to be that long. You could have something a little bit longer if you're doing an in-depth tutorial or detailed information on a specific subject.

BONUS TIP #1

Make your videos a little more fancy with a custom video intro. You can do that on a website called Fiverr.com for just $5-$10. Having a consistent look and feel is going to take your video to the next level and look very professional.

Paralyzed by FEAR

Many people have the idea of shooting videos and they know they should shoot videos. But for whatever reason, they never actually get in front of the camera.

People plan and decide what they're going to do and they script it out and they do all this research. And then the whole day goes by and they never make the video.

Just get on camera and do it.

Treat a video shoot like a live event.

Don't go back and reshoot a million times.

Even if you stumble and bumble – you go back and look at some of my videos, and I look a little silly in some of them. But it doesn't matter to me because that's just who I am, and I was going to keep it natural and I was going to go with it. Whatever comes out comes out.

Just like a live event where you can't stop and pause and go back, treat the video the exact same way and just do it.

Just knock it out and get it done.

Done is better than perfect.

You'll get better and better as you go, just like with anything else.

Chapter 3 | Publish

Now we're going to do some basic SEO, or Search Engine Optimization. Now the reality is SEO is unsexy. But it is very necessary. This is how we're going to actually get people to find your videos.

Instead of just putting your video on YouTube as IMG-02-2013 or whatever the title was in your phone or camera, we're going to make sure we change everything so that somebody can actually find our video.

There's a 5-step process within the search engine optimization even.

1. FILE NAME

Hook up your camera or phone to the computer so we can move the video onto the desktop. Before you upload the video to YouTube, change the title by right clicking on the video and click RENAME. Change it to the keyword phrase you want to rank.

2. VIDEO TITLE

We want to change the title to the same phrase. YouTube will let you put a really long title but you want to keep titles under 70 characters. 60 characters or less is even better.

3. VIDEO DESCRIPTION

We want to make sure that we have the same phrase in the description. Here you can write out some call to action or add some text about the video.

4. KEYWORDS

We add the same phrase and each word individually in the tags underneath the description on YouTube when we upload the video.

5. WEBSITE/CALL TO ACTION

The last step in optimizing the video is to put a website link at the beginning of the description. The reason we want to do that is, number one, it creates a link to your website, so that's important.

And number two, once we get this video to rank on the first page of Google, your website address is going to be right there on the first page of Google for people to see.

It's a great tactic of getting your website seen more often by putting it at the very beginning of your description.

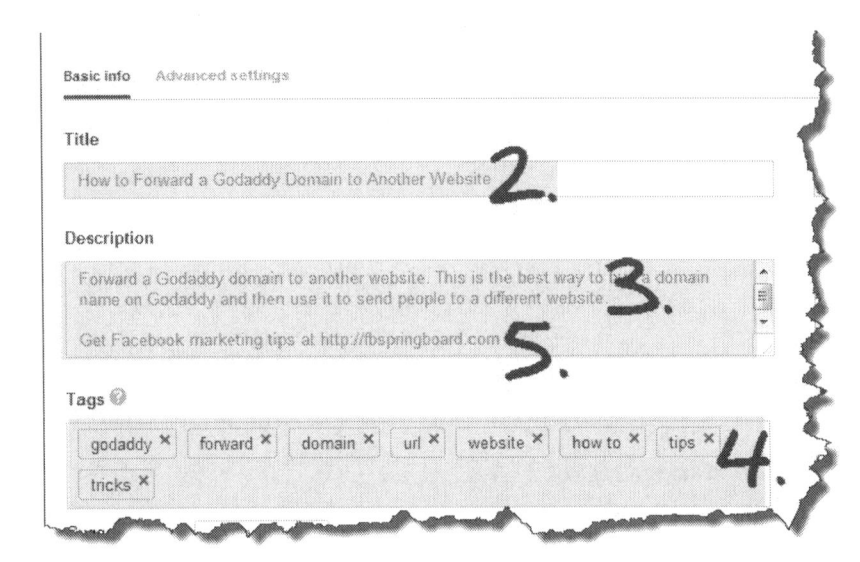

Ultimately, YouTube is looking at the video title, description, keyword tags and then listening to the video to make sure it actually has to do with that topic.

That's how YouTube decides what to rank for different searches.

A lot of times when people go to put a video on YouTube, they want to put "Nick's Social Tip" or whatever, because they want it to be about them or they want to brand a certain way.

Nobody's looking for that on YouTube. At least not in the beginning but you can train people what to search for.

What most YouTube viewers are looking for is how to solve problems.

Be purposeful with how you title your stuff.

Brand yourself once somebody is in your videos, once they've seen your content, brand yourself there.

Don't try to brand yourself in the titles and in the description too much.

Just get people to watch your content; click on your call to action; and get in contact with you.

That's what's important.

Publishing Videos

Go after one specific phrase per video.

- Same phrase in title, tags, & description.

- 5-20 tags. Don't go crazy. Keep them relevant.

- YouTube rewards longer content because it gets longer view time & time on the site.

Chapter 4 | Connect

The next piece you want to do is go to your website, to your blog – and hopefully, that's on Wordpress.

We will create a blog post.

We could just share the video and have everyone watch it on YouTube; but why give YouTube that much credit?

I'm happy that people find my videos on YouTube but I'm more interested in getting people to my website.

Ultimately, everything that we're going to do, everything we're doing through social media, through search engine optimization, through video marketing, all those things are attraction hooks and stuff to get people back to our fishing pond.

The fishing pond is your website, it's your blog.

That's where you want to get people to.

The faster we can get them there, the better.

It's great to put your stuff on YouTube and different video sites. I definitely recommend that because you drive people back to your website. If you can get them directly to your website, it's even better because you've just eliminated that extra step.

The best way to drive traffic is to write a blog post about the same topic as your video.

We're going to create a blog and we're going to title it the same way as we've titled our video.

The ideal post size is going to be around 350 words.

Now a few people are going to say that's intimidating, especially if you're not writing that much at the moment.

As a minimum, you can do 200-300 words, that's easy. You can do a 300 word blog in 15 minutes.

On a maximum, I'm going to say 500-800 words. If you get over that, it starts to get a little bit wordy. People may not read the whole thing; so about 350 words is ideal.

After you have the blog post written, go over to the video on YouTube. Down below the video is a little button that says share.

If you click on share, there's another button that says embed the video.

Embed just means you're going to display the video on a different website.

What you want to do is you want to embed your YouTube video inside the blog post.

This just means the video will be visible and people can watch it on your website without going to YouTube.

YouTube Embed Code

Make sure your blog article is unique content. Do not steal (copy and paste) other people's content.

Please do not steal from Google or steal somebody else's blog post and copy and paste it as your own.

I'm not saying you can't go out there and see what other people are doing and "get inspired" – that's perfectly fine.

Don't just copy and paste it.

They will figure it out. You don't want to deal with that. So make sure it's unique content.

You know what; some people are going to say they're not interested in writing blogs or I'm not a blogger.

Do you prefer to get the results from blogging without all the research, writing, posting, and promoting?

Shoot me an email with the subject "Monthly Blog Package" to nick@legionofloanofficers.com and tell me what city you are in and a link to your website. I'll reply with our package options.

We have world class copywriters on staff who are creating high quality content on a weekly or monthly basis for different mortgage and real estate clients all around the United States.

Chapter 5 | Promote

Now it's time to get social. You want to share the blog post out on social media.

If you have a profile, share it.

So whether you have a profile on Facebook, Twitter, LinkedIn, and Instagram, wherever it is, you want to make sure that you're sharing a link back to your blog on those sites.

Everybody knows how to share on Facebook, Twitter, and LinkedIn.

BONUS TIP #2

Use Zapier.com to automate different tasks with blogs and sharing to social media. It's a self explanatory setup with a lot of integrated services. And it's free!

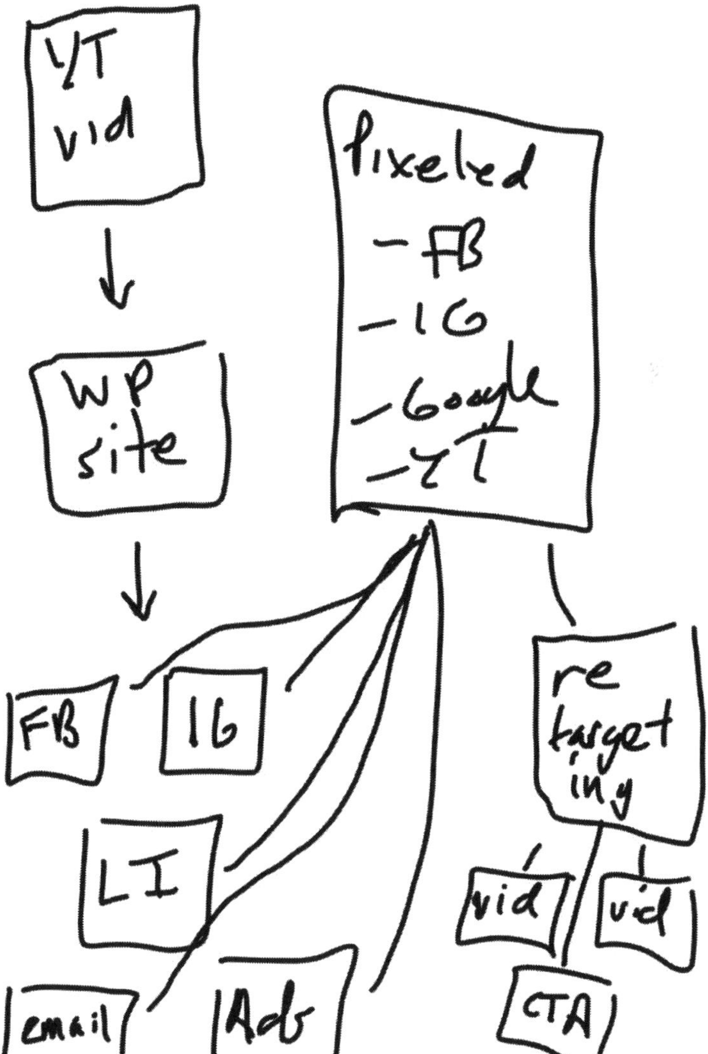

Y/T vid
WP site
Pixeled
-FB
-IG
-Google
-YT
FB
IG
LI
email
Ads
re target ing
vid
vid
CTA

Conclusion

This whole Page One Takeover thing is a pretty simple 5 step process but you have to actually do the work.

That seems to be the break down for most people is they get excited for a short period and then they stop.

Every step is important in the process if you want to rank your videos on the first page of Google.

You've got to do the **research** first.

You've got to **shoot** the video.

You've got to do the **SEO** and you've got to keyword it.

It's the unsexiest part of what we are doing but also probably the most important since it's telling YouTube and Google exactly what the video is about.

Next, write the **blog post**, embed the YouTube video and then share the blog post out through your **social media** accounts and **email list**.

It's really that simple to take over Google with free videos.

Commit to the work and watch what happens.

You might overestimate what you can do in one month and underestimate what you can do in one year.

Stay the course.

Bonus Content | How To Rank Your Cell Phone Number As a YouTube Video To Get More Call Backs and Conversations

This 15 minute process will pay you back for months and years to come.

What do people do when they get a call from an unknown phone number?

Lots of them Google the number to find out who it is. Do you do that?

This will get a video ranked on Google page 1 so it's always crystal clear who you are when they go to check.

1. Record The Video

Here's a basic script you can use for this video. It needs to be at least 30 seconds long.

Shoot it on your cell phone as a horizontal (sideways) video.

"Did you Google 555-444-3322? That's me, Full Name, a TITLE right here in

City. I could have been calling you back from a Facebook or YouTube ad or maybe you reached out some other way and I was returning your call. Feel free to call me back at 555-444-3322 or answer next time you see my number pop up. Have a great one."

2. Upload It To YouTube

Go into the YouTube app on your phone and upload the video. As of publishing, it's a camera icon with a + in the top menu. Find the video you want to upload from your camera roll and hit next.

3. Add The Title and Description

First, here's the title template to follow –

555-444-3333 (5554443333) is Nick Carpenter, a Denver Mortgage Broker.

555-444-3333 (5554443333) is Full Name, A City Title.

Next, we'll add a video description following the same basic template –

Did you Google 555-444-3333 or 5554443333? That's me, Full Name, a City Title. http://Link.com

Did you Google 555-444-3333 or 5554443333? That's me, Nick Carpenter, a Denver Mortgage Broker. http://Link.com

Hit next and let the video finish uploading as an Unlisted Video or Private Video to YouTube.

4. Add Video Tags

Once the video is uploaded, click your profile icon in the top right corner and open your channel. Go to the full list of videos and you can click the 3 dots to open a menu allowing you to edit the video.

Add the following tags and no more, replacing your number with the fake one: 555-444-3333, 5554443333, your full name, City, State.

Hit the SAVE button and wait an hour to check on Google and see if the video is ranking.

If this works, can you do me a huge favor and make a video about it and email it to nick@legionofloanofficers.com and I'll send you a gift.

You can also post online and tag me and include a photo of the book so other people can learn this too.

I grew up all over the U.S. as a military brat and went on to serve in the Air Force for 6 years. My enlistment included a tour in Iraq where our base was attacked over 100 times in 6 months.

In 2005, I completed my Air Force service and began my next chapter as a real estate agent where I was honored to win rookie of the year. This led to my love of marketing and lead generation which I have been focused on for the past decade.

Today I work with Mortgage Brokers and Loan Officers who want to use online marketing to grow their business, get more leads, and make life easier inside **The Legion of Loan Officers**.

Connect with me online:

Facebook - fb.com/nillanick

YouTube - fb.com/nillanicktv

Instagram - instagram.com/beardedmarketer

Resources:

Legion of Loan Officers | America's mastermind for smart mortgage professionals - legionofloanofficers.com

KLTCRM | World's simplest CRM - kltcrm.com

Adsmiths | Modern Day Propagandists - adsmiths.co

LoanTees | Up your mortgage swag - loantees.com

Made in the USA
Coppell, TX
17 August 2021